Opposite Cathedral Square, in the very centre of Christchurch, is dominated by the Anglican cathedral and its 65.5-metre spire. The building was designed in Great Britain by Sir George Gilbert Scott, a renowned Gothic Revival architect, and construction took place from 1864 to 1904. The contrasting 21st-century sculpture *Chalice* is the work of Neil Dawson. The leaf patterns represent the trees that grew in the area when European settlers arrived aboard the First Four Ships in December 1850.

Right The Italianate former Chief Post Office was completed in 1879, but these days it serves as an information centre. The statue nearby is of John Robert Godley, first leader of the Canterbury settlement. Godley named the new town after the Christ Church College he attended in Oxford, England.

Below The long-serving Wizard is integral to Cathedral Square. He is frequently heard taunting listeners with outlandish philosophy tinged with dollops of truth.

Previous pages The cathedral that gave Christchurch's main square its name is a church for all people, seating a thousand worshippers. Apart from its obvious beauty, the building displays a wealth of Canterbury heritage.

Left At noon in Cathedral Square the colourful town crier announces the day's events.

Below Oblivious to tram bells and other disturbances, regular chess players while away the hours in the centre of Christchurch.

Opposite Tram No. 178, the Brill, prepares to depart Cathedral Square. Once home to a number of cinemas, the square these days has but one, the Regent Theatre. The domed building opened in May 1905 as the Royal Exchange. Celebrations marking the opening of Christchurch's electric tramways were held in the Royal Café on the second floor in the following month.

Opposite The Bridge of Remembrance was dedicated on Armistice Day 1924. It was built as a memorial to New Zealand servicemen who died in World War I, and replaced the Cashel Street bridge over which the servicemen had marched before they left for overseas.

Above The Bridge of Remembrance is linked to the tram by the City Mall and that part of Oxford Terrace known as the Strip, an avenue of cafés and bars beside the Avon.

Right At the corner of Worcester Boulevard and Cambridge Terrace is the sprawling Canterbury Club. It was built in 1874 as a gentlemen's club — but it has recently become a ladies' and gentlemen's club.

Following pages No. 178 crosses Montreal Street beside the Christchurch Art Gallery, which opened in 2003. The glass façade depicts the flow of the Avon through the city, while Graham Bennett's sculpture *Reasons for Voyaging* suggests in its angular steel booms the journeys that have brought all New Zealanders to this country. The gallery's Maori name, Te Puna o Waiwhetu, which means 'wellspring of water reflecting the stars', was given by the local iwi or tribe, Ngai Tahu.

These pages Covering 2.5 hectares, the Arts Centre is a thriving inner-city facility known for performing arts, craft shops and weekend markets. From 1877 to 1976 it was the campus of Canterbury University, boasting such students as Ernest Rutherford, nuclear scientist; Apirana Ngata, New Zealand's first Maori graduate; Helen Connon, the British Empire's first woman honours graduate; Ngaio Marsh, crime writer; and William Pickering, NASA space scientist.

Boxcar No. 11 pauses at the Galleria stop (left). The Tudor-style former student union building (top) is now a bustling seafood and vegetarian café with a popular in-house brewery. And even amid the busy weekend markets (bottom) it's possible to find a quiet spot to ponder a good book.

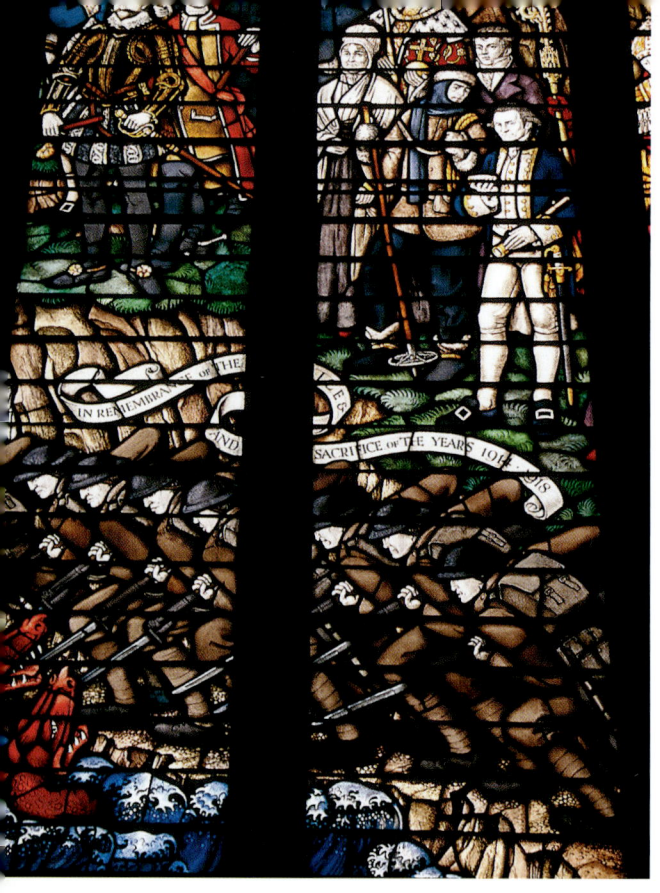

Left and below The Great Hall, where Canterbury University students once attended graduation ceremonies and lectures, provides a grand tramway exit from Worcester Boulevard into Rolleston Avenue. Designed by Benjamin Mountfort and completed in 1882, it now serves as a function centre. It is perhaps best known for its poignant stained-glass window, which was unveiled in 1938 as a memorial to students and staff who perished in World War I.

Opposite top The Antigua Boatsheds of 1882 are the only commercial boatsheds remaining on the Avon — there have in the past been as many as six places hiring out boats.

Opposite bottom Elegant punts based at the Antigua Boatsheds glide through the tranquil woodlands of the Christchurch Botanic Gardens. The name Avon was given to the river by Scottish farming pioneers William and John Deans. They named it after the Kilmarnock Avon, a tributary of the Clyde in Ayrshire.

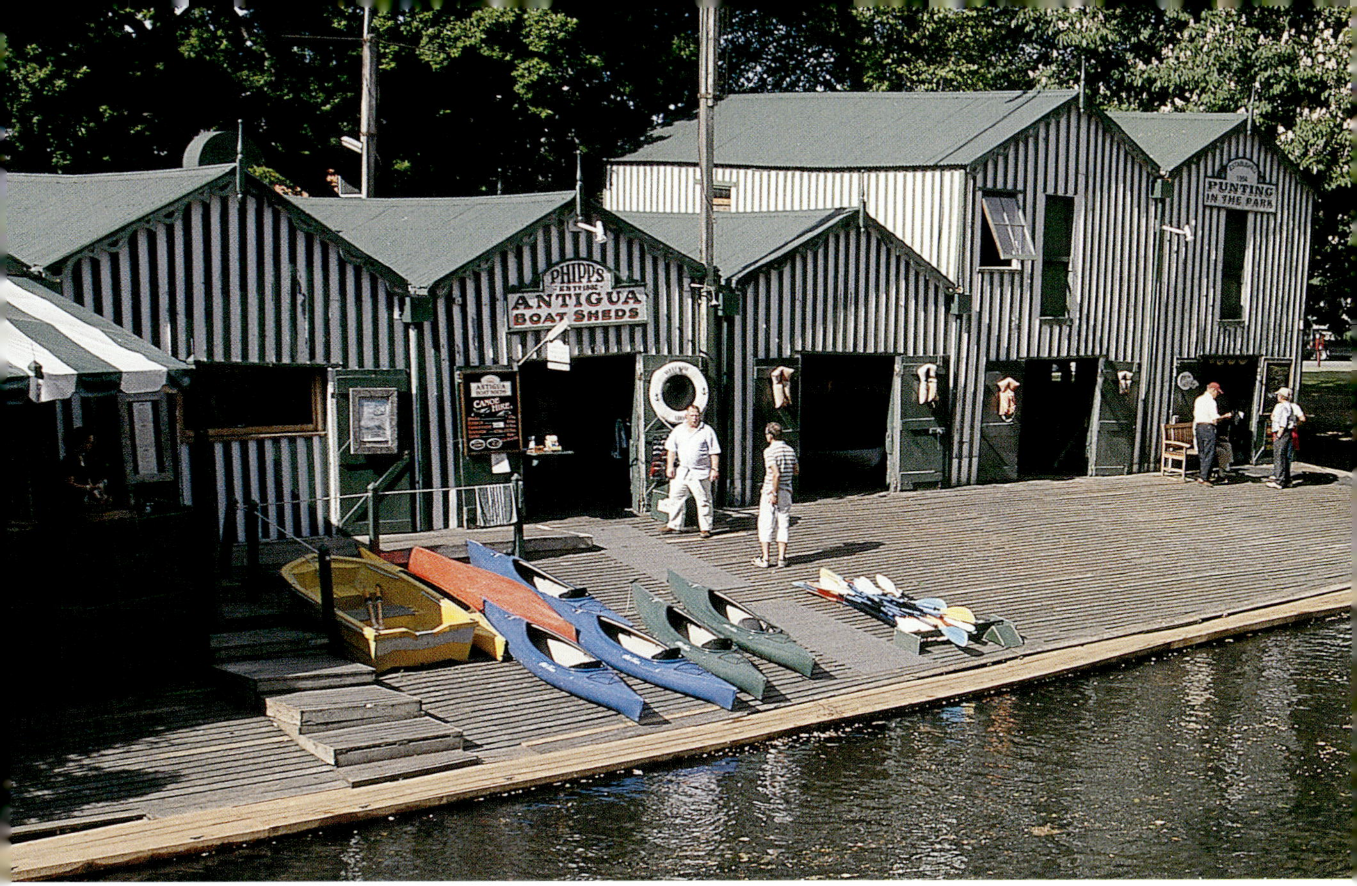
PHIPPS
ANTIGUA
BOAT SHEDS
ANTIGUA
CANOE HIRE.
PUNTING
IN THE PARK

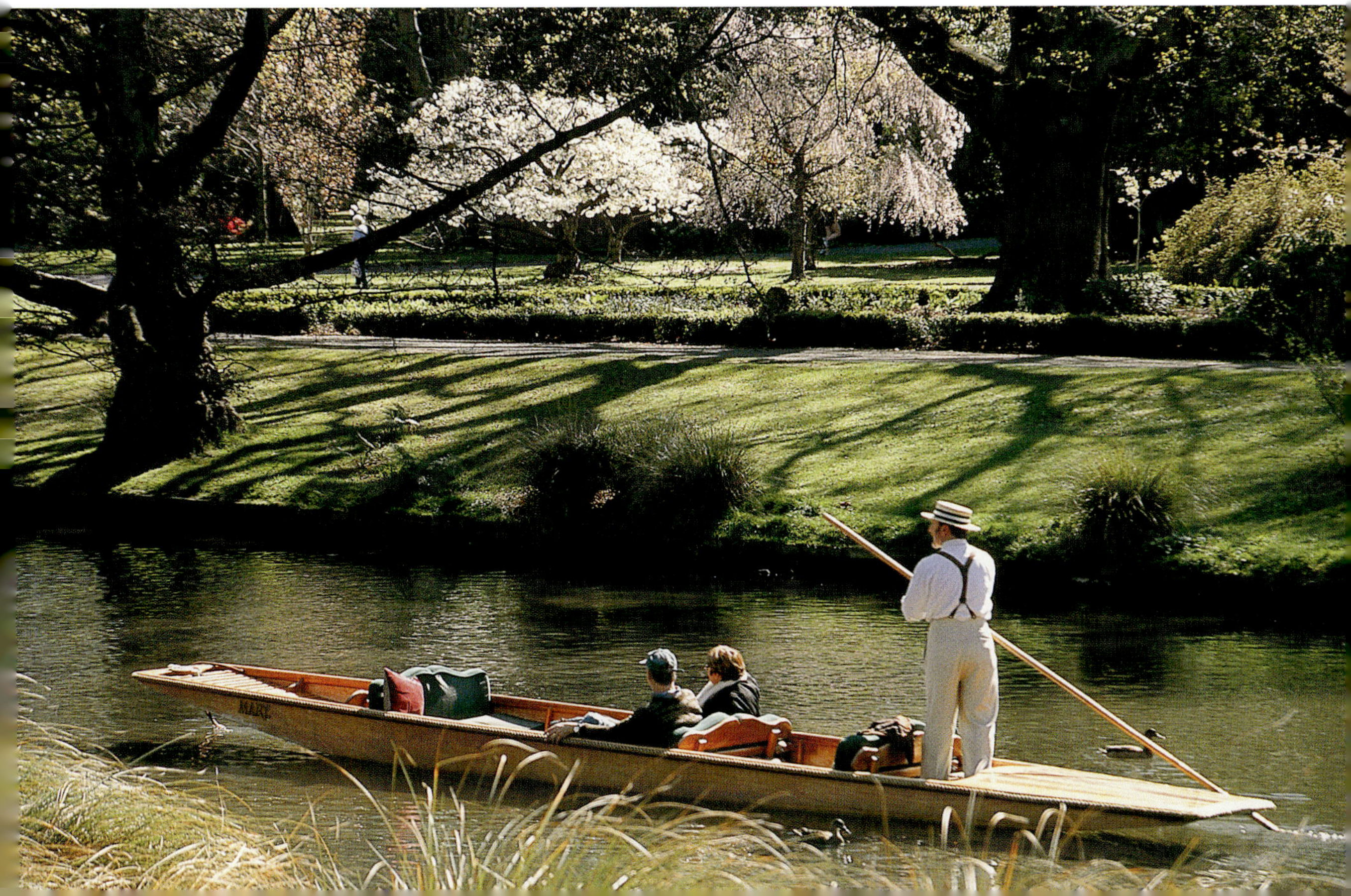

Above Tram No. 244 turns in to Rolleston Avenue, passing Canterbury Museum. The elegant building opened in 1870. Its inaugural director, Julius von Haast from Bonn in Germany, donated the nucleus of an excellent collection.

Left The Antarctic Wing of the museum features the farm tractor Sir Edmund Hillary drove to the South Pole in 1958. Christchurch was the usual base for early Antarctic exploration, including expeditions led by Ernest Shackleton and Robert Falcon Scott.

Opposite top The Christchurch Botanic Gardens, established in 1863, are often voted among the world's best. This lush spring view looks towards the Arts Centre.

Opposite bottom left The Edwardian Peacock Fountain, in the botanic gardens, was donated by the Hon. J. T. Peacock and cast at the Coalbrookdale foundry in Shropshire, England.

Opposite bottom right A model yacht club has sailed its boats on Lake Victoria in Hagley Park since the 1890s. Miniature regattas are held on Wednesdays and Saturdays.

Previous pages A burst of spring in Hagley Park woodlands. Covering 186 hectares, Hagley is one of the world's largest inner-city parks. The name is taken from Hagley Hall, the English home of early Canterbury Association representative Lord Lyttelton.

Opposite Founded in 1850 and modelled on English public schools, Christ's College is one of New Zealand's best-known educational institutions. The chapel-like Big School, built in 1863, is still in use as a library.

Above The Venetian-Gothic former Christchurch Girls' High School (1881–1986) is in Cranmer Square. Helen Connon, appointed principal in 1882, encouraged young women to become scholars rather than simply home makers.

Right One of the finest city interiors is found in the 1862 debating chamber of the old Canterbury Provincial Council buildings on Durham Street. The decorative barrel-vaulted ceiling was painted by Frenchman J. C. St Quentin. It is said he was hoisted to work each morning with his brushes and paints, as well as a necessary bottle of cognac.

Left In Victoria Square, this statue commemorates James Cook, who in 1769 became the first European to circumnavigate New Zealand.

Below Every few minutes the trams rattle across the Armagh Street bridge.

Opposite top Punts ply the river next to Victoria Square, passing the Ferrier Fountain and Christchurch's town hall. Originally called Market Place and known as the commercial centre of the city, the square was renamed with the unveiling of a statue of Queen Victoria in 1903.

Opposite bottom The Hamish Hay bridge is a pedestrian walkway leading to the Crowne Plaza Hotel in Victoria Square. First opened in 1864, it served as a road and tram bridge before the redevelopment of the square in the late 1980s. With extensive grass and fountains, the open space now offers recreation and rejuvenation for city workers.

Opposite and above Street events are a treat for Christchurch citizens and visitors. Roads are closed for the annual Santa Parade and even tram staff have time to enjoy the sounds of a passing brass band. Other summer highlights include the World Buskers Festival and the Festival of Flowers and Romance.

Right When trams resume running after the parade, there is always a pram to be returned to its owner. Carrying prams on hooks on the front of public transport was unique to Christchurch. The practice continued when buses replaced trams in 1954. Only the newest Metro buses, providing interior luggage storage, are without the once obligatory pram hooks.

Left Johnson's Grocers is a short stroll along Colombo Street from the Victoria Square tram stop. Since it opened early last century little seems to have changed in the shop, where sugar and tea are still weighed as in former times.

Below Boutique shops and cafés are a delightful feature of the City Loop. Many are found in New Regent Street, which is dedicated to pedestrians and trams. The mirror-image Spanish Mission architecture was the choice of architect H. Francis Willis, who in 1932 decided to give the city a street of bright colours. The builder, Peter Graham, was a Londoner, hence the New Regent Street name.

Opposite Cathedral Junction emulates a grand English railway terminal. The junction was the brainchild of property developer John Britten, who was also known for his very fast and beautifully made motorbikes. Despite Britten's untimely death in 1995, the project has been completed with many of the decorative features inspired by him. There are cafés and restaurants with outdoor seating, speciality shops and the Tram Station store. Next stop is Cathedral Square, the beginning of the City Loop.

These pages The city by night is a special place, especially when viewed from a tram. The Christchurch Tramway Restaurant, aboard tram No. 411, offers all the opulence of the Orient Express (opposite top left). As the tram cruises darkening streets, the clinking of glasses is complemented by the clanging of the motorman's bell. Outside, a kaleidoscope of lights includes the dandelion-shapes of the Ferrier Fountain (opposite top right) and the Hamish Hay bridge (opposite bottom) in Victoria Square. A diner's quick eye will spot the Christchurch casino (right), which in 1994 became the first official casino in New Zealand. Occasionally the tram will pause on Worcester Boulevard bridge (below).

Electric tramcars made their debut in Christchurch on 5 June 1905, and the last trams ran on 11 September 1954. The present Christchurch Tramway, owned by the Wood Scenic Line Ltd, was the brainchild of the Tramway Historical Society and a visionary Christchurch City Council. Power is from a 600V DC overhead wire, and trams run on standard gauge 4 foot 8½ inch track.

Boxcar No. 11 was built by J. G. Brill & Co. of Philadelphia in 1903 for the opening of electric tramways in Dunedin. It spent many years as a leaky shed before being restored by the Tramway Historical Society and returned to service on the society's tramway at Ferrymead Heritage Park in 1974.

Boon No. 152 was built in Christchurch by Boon & Co. for the Christchurch Tramway Board in 1910 and operated until 1952. A 44-seat double-saloon tramcar, it has a drop-centre open section, a layout later adopted in Melbourne. In a first for a tramway museum, the Peckham maximum traction bogies were built from scratch at Ferrymead Heritage Park.

Brill No. 178 is another Christchurch Tramway Board car, built in 1921 by Boon & Co. It was converted to one-man operation during the 1930s depression. In 1970 it became the first electric tram restored at Ferrymead.

Melbourne No. 244 was built by the Melbourne Metropolitan Tramway Board in 1925 as a double-truck 52-seater. It ran for almost 60 years before coming to Christchurch.

Melbourne No. 411 is the restaurant tram. Built in 1927, it is a W2 class similar to No. 244. It was withdrawn from the MMTB in 1982 and converted into a colonial-style dining car by the Sydney Tramway Museum.

Two trailers are also in use. Duckhouse No. 115, a 4-wheel trailer seating 28 passengers, was built by Boon & Co. in 1908. It is frequently coupled to the Boon No. 152. Trailer No. 18, known as the Dunedin Horse Tram, was built in 187 by Guthrie Larnach and is the oldest vehicle in the fleet. It is teamed up with the Boxcar No. 11.

These pages Tram drivers (motormen) such as Owen and Mary offer commentaries for passengers. The restored interiors and exteriors display painstaking craftsmanship. Off duty trams stay in the barn in Tramway Lane.

CHRISTCHURCH
TRAMWAY BOARD

152
BOON & CO., MAKERS, CH.CH.N.Z.

No 18

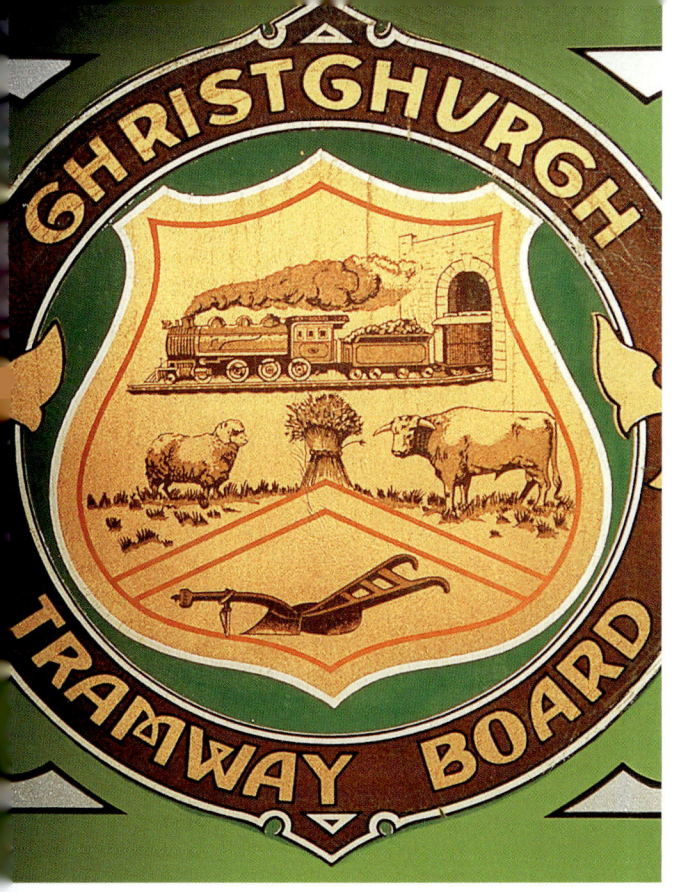

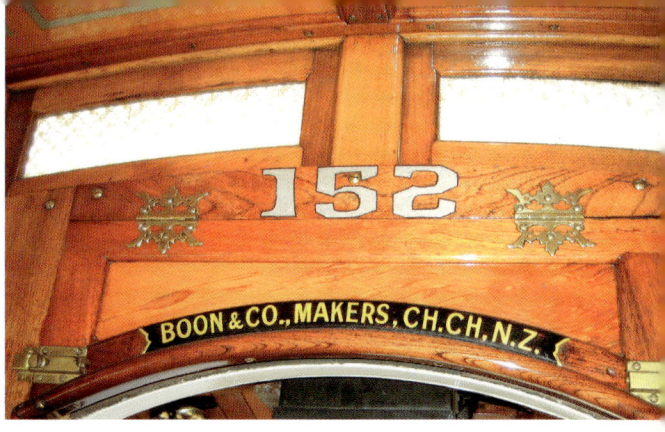

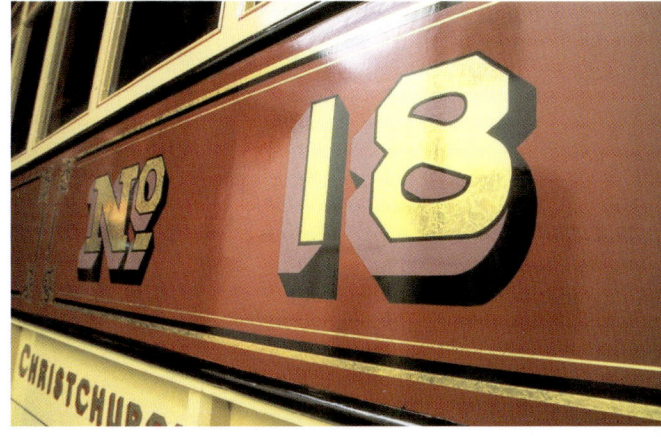

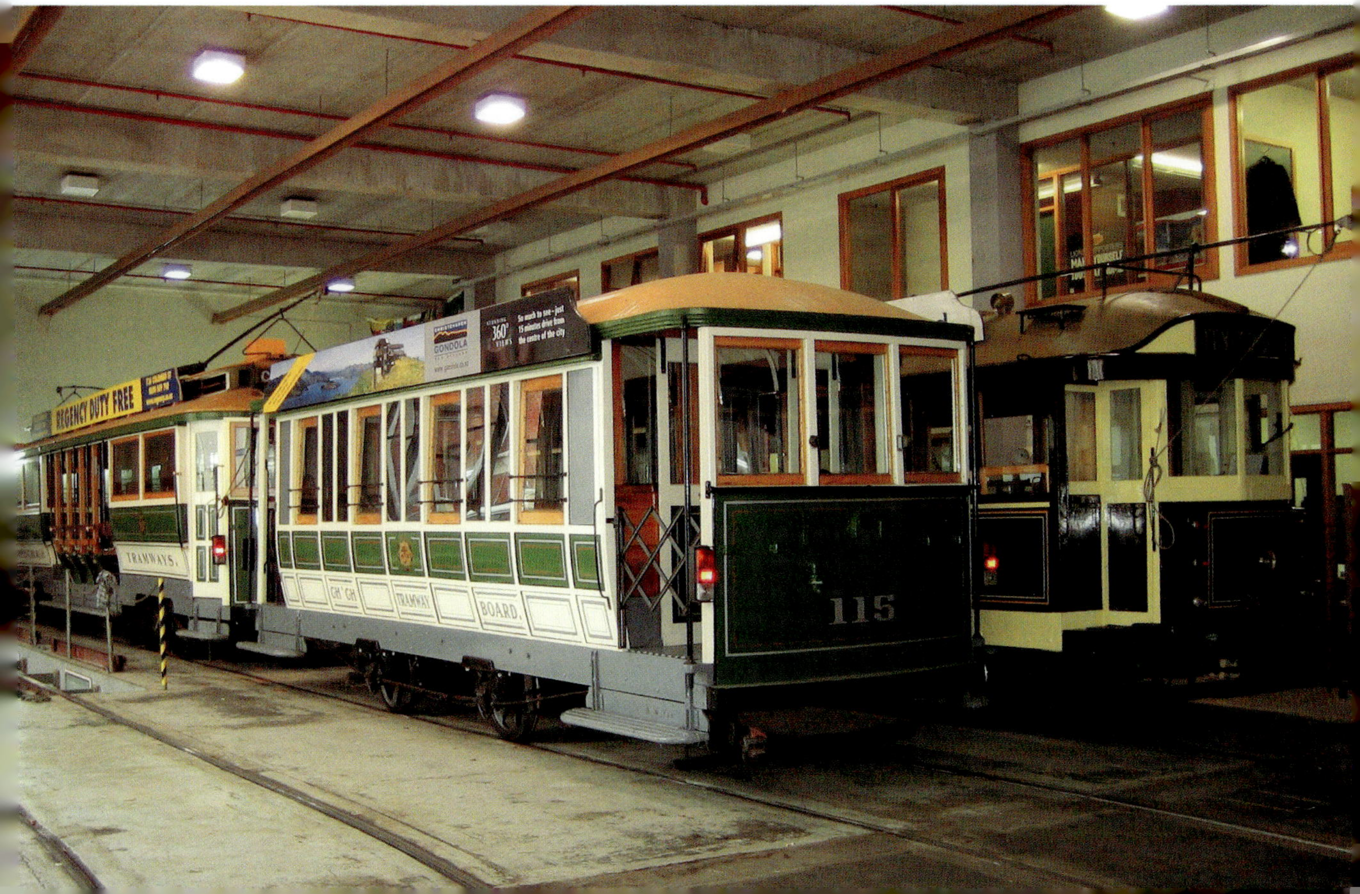
REGENCY DUTY FREE
GONDOLA
TRAMWAYS.
CH'CH TRAMWAY BOARD.
115